FEB 2 3 2005

DATE DUE

OCT 3 1 2005	
MAY 0 2 2015	

DEMCO, INC. 38-2931

Uncharted, Unexplored, and Unexplained

Scientific Advancements of the 19th Century

Dmitri Mendeleyev
and the Periodic Table

Mitchell Lane
PUBLISHERS

P.O. Box 196
Hockessin, Delaware
19707

Uncharted, Unexplored, and Unexplained

Scientific Advancements of the 19th Century

Titles in the Series

Visit us on the web: www.mitchelllane.com
Comments? email us: mitchelllane@mitchelllane.com

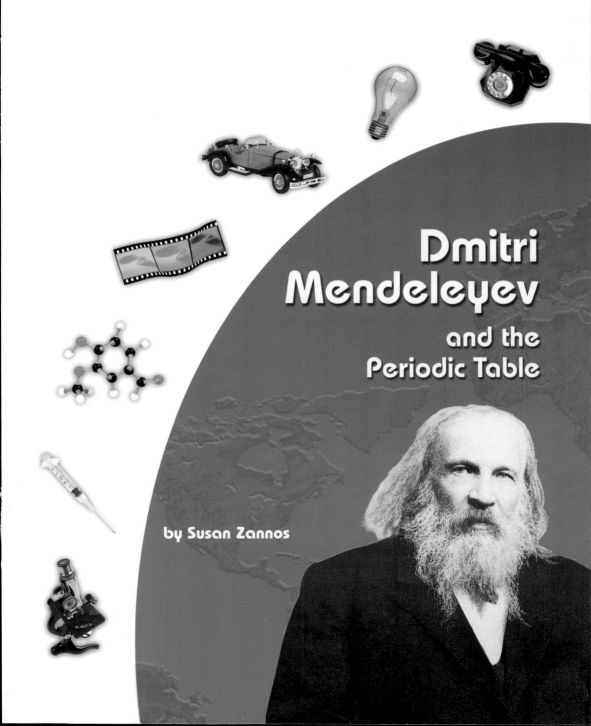

Dmitri
Mendeleyev

and the
Periodic Table

by Susan Zannos

Uncharted, Unexplored, and Unexplained

Scientific Advancements of the 19th Century

Copyright © 2005 by Mitchell Lane Publishers, Inc. All rights reserved. No part of this book may be reproduced without written permission from the publisher. Printed and bound in the United States of America.

Printing   1   2   3   4   5   6   7   8

Library of Congress Cataloging-in-Publication Data
Zannos, Susan
        Dmitri Mendeleyev and the periodic table / Susan Zannos
        p. cm. — (Uncharted, unexplored & unexplained : scientific advancements of the 19th century)
Includes bibliographical references and index.
        ISBN 1-58415-267-2 (lib bdg.)
1. Mendeleyev Dmitry Ivanovich. 1834 - 1907—Juvenile literature. 2. Chemists—Russia (Federation)—Biography. 3. Periodic law—Tables—Juvenile literature. 4. Chemical elements—Juvenile literature. [1. Mendeleyev Dmitry Ivanovich. 1834 - 1907. 2. Chemists. 3. Scientists 4. Periodic law —Tables. 4. Chemical elements.] I. Title. II. Uncharted, unexplored & unexplained.
QD22.M3 z36 2004
540'.92—dc22

2002022143

ABOUT THE AUTHOR: **Susan Zannos** has been a lifelong educator, having taught at all levels, from preschool to college, in Mexico, Greece, Italy, Russia and Lithuania, as well as in the United States. She has published a mystery *Trust the Liar* (Walker and Co.) and *Human Types: Essence and the Ennegram* (Samuel Weiser). Her book *Human Types* was recently translated into Russian and in 2003 Susan was invited to tour Russia and lecture about her book. Another book she wrote for young adults, *Careers in Education* (Mitchell Lane) was selected for the New York Public Library's "Books for the Teen Age 2003 List." She has written many books for children, including *Chester Carlson and the Development of Xerography* and *The Life and Times of Ludwig van Beethoven* (Mitchell Lane). When not traveling, Susan lives in the Sierra Foothills of Norhern California.

PHOTO CREDITS: Cover: Corbis; p. 6 Science Photo; p. 9 Hulton/Archive; p.14 Getty; pp. 18-19 Hulton/Archive; p. 22 Corbis; pp. 28, 34 Science Photo.

PUBLISHER'S NOTE: This story is based on the author's extensive research, which she believes to be accurate. Documentation of such research is contained on page 47. The story in the first chapter is based on well researched fact; however, the dialogue is fictional.

The internet sites referenced herein were active as of the publication date. Due to the fleeting nature of some web sites, we cannot guarantee they will all be active when you are reading this book.

Unaltered, Unexplored, and Unexplained

Scientific Advancements of the 19th Century

Dmitri Mendeleyev

and the Periodic Table

*For Your Information

In spite of a serious illness, Dmitri Mendeleyev won the gold medal for best student of the year in 1825 and qualified as a teacher in the Crimea. The following year he completed his master's thesis and began lecturing about chemistry in St. Petersburg.

1

Fire!

Mitia woke suddenly. Something was wrong. Church bells were pealing frantically. People were shouting. The usual dull red glow on his bedroom wall from the glass factory at night was now a bright light that lit up the whole room. The boy stumbled from his bed to the window. Tongues of orange flame licked at the black Siberian night and reflected from the snow. The glass factory was burning!

"Mother?" he called.

Mitia struggled into his trousers and jacket and ran to the front door. Behind him he heard his sister Elizabeth calling to him. "Mitia, what is it? What's happening?"

"Fire," he said as he put on his boots. "The glass factory!" He rushed out the door and joined the neighbors who were running toward the burning building. He found his mother among the people silently watching the flames. It was clear there was nothing that could be done.

Fourteen-year-old Mitia and his mother, Maria, stood side by side. They did not speak. They stood there watching the walls crumble and the flames gradually die down, long after the other villagers of Aremziansk had returned to their homes and their beds. The glass factory, which Maria had managed, had been the support of their large family. Its destruction meant financial ruin.

Maria Dmitrievna Korniliev was a remarkable woman. The Korniliev family was prominent in the nearby Siberian capital of Tobolsk. Descended from the fiery Tatars who had invaded Russia from Asia centuries before, the Kornilievs had brought to Siberia both papermaking and glassmaking; Maria's father had introduced the printing press and started the first newspaper in Siberia. Maria married Ivan Pavlovitch Mendeleyev, a prominent educator and director of the local gymnasium, which is what secondary schools were called. Ivan and Maria had 14 children.

Soon after the youngest boy, Mitia, was born, Ivan became blind. Maria had to support their large family. To help her, Maria's family offered her the position of manager at their glass factory in Aremziansk. In 1848, the year of the disastrous fire, two children were left at home, Mitia and his frail older sister Elizabeth.

In the days following the fire, there were family meetings to discuss what should be done. There were also angry discussions about what had started the fire. Some thought it had been arson, that workers inspired by the radical ideas sweeping Europe had deliberately burned the factory. Others thought it had been an accident resulting from a carelessly supervised glass furnace. They would never know.

What the family did know was that there was no money to rebuild the factory. The only money left was the amount Maria had been able to save for her youngest son's education.

"The family needs that money, Maria," her brother said. "It belongs to all of us. It came from our factory."

"No," she said firmly. "It is for Mitia's schooling."

"He doesn't do all that well in school," her eldest son pointed out. "If he got good grades it might be different. He won't even be accepted to a university."

The art of glassblowing has changed very little since it fascinated young Dmitri Mendeleyev in his family's glass factory in Siberia. It inspired the master's thesis that he completed in 1856, "Expansion of Substances Due to Heat." In this photograph taken in 1934, a glassblower is creating an amber glass bowl.

Maria just shook her head. She knew that Mitia was brilliant, even if he wasn't doing well in some of his classes. The only member of the family who shared her opinion was her daughter Olga's husband, Bessargin, who had tutored Mitia and knew the boy had an exceptional mind.

Maria had a talk with her son. "Dmitri," she began, and he knew that she was serious when she called him Dmitri, "you will have to study much harder. You will have to get top marks in history and in Latin and Greek. . . . "

"But mother, they are stupid and boring. What sense is there in learning a language nobody speaks? Who cares about things that happened hundreds of years ago? There's a whole world to be discovered in science. Bessargin says . . ."

"Yes, Bessargin is so smart he got himself exiled to Siberia. Listen to what I say: If you do not get good marks in all your classes you will never be admitted to the university in Moscow. And that is where you are going."

"Moscow! How will I get to Moscow?"

"We will get there. And when we do you need to be ready to pass the entrance examinations for the university."

Mitia did study hard. He studied the mathematics and science that he loved. He studied Russian because it was the language of his country and his people. And he studied history and classical languages out of respect for his mother's tireless efforts to support their family and because of her dreams for him. But he still hated these subjects and considered them useless. Over 50 years later he would write:

"We could live at the present day without a Plato, but a double number of Newtons is required to discover the secrets of nature, and to bring life into harmony with the laws of nature." [1]

Despite his resistance, Dmitri did get good grades in all of his classes. He completed his studies at the gymnasium in 1849. As soon as he graduated, his mother loaded their few possessions into a small horse-drawn wagon. With Mitia and Elizabeth, her youngest daughter, Maria Dmitrievna Korniliev began the difficult 1,400-mile journey to Moscow.

All through the hot, dry summer they traveled. Sometimes kind peasant families would give them a simple meal and shelter at the end of a long day. More often they were far from any villages when night fell, and slept out under the Siberian stars. Crossing the Ural Mountains they had to walk, carrying as much as they could to spare their horse. Often they could cover no more than 10 miles in a day so that the poor animal could rest and feed. After crossing the mountains they were in a more heavily populated area of Russia. Other travelers helped them as much as they could, giving Maria and Elizabeth rides while Mitia followed with the wagon.

At last they reached Moscow. Maria and Dmitri dressed in their best clothes and, taking the records of his successful studies, went to Moscow University to enroll. The university had a quota system for admitting students from the provinces. But Siberia was a new province. No quota had been set for students from Siberia. Their application was refused. Mother and son went to other institutions of higher education in Moscow. At each one they were told the same thing: Fifteen-year-old Dmitri Mendeleyev's Siberian qualifications were not recognized in Moscow.

Maria repacked the wagon. They set out on the road again, this time headed 400 miles north to St. Petersburg. At the University of St. Petersburg they were told the same thing they had been told in Moscow: No students from Siberia could be admitted. Again Maria went from institution to institution, looking for a school that would allow Dmitri to enroll. Everywhere she was turned down. She was running out of possibilities. She was exhausted and her health was failing, but she kept going.

The morning she entered the offices of the Central Pedagogical Institute, a training college for high school teachers, she was so tired she could hardly stand. She sank gratefully into the chair offered her by the head of the school, who looked over Dmitri's records.

"It seems that the boy has a good academic background," the man said. "Unfortunately we cannot accept candidates from Siberia since . . . Wait. Mendeleyev? Do you by any chance know Ivan Pavlovitch Mendeleyev?"

"He was my husband. Dmitri's father. He died two years ago."

"I am so sorry," the head of the college said. "We were classmates together at this very school. We were good friends, but we lost touch through the years. I'm certain that we will be able to find a place for Ivan's son if he can pass the entrance exams." He stopped, realizing that Maria was close to tears of joy. "I think," he went on softly, "there is some scholarship money available for such a promising student."

The Romanov czars were the absolute rulers of Russia. Theirs was the largest empire in the world during the 19th century. Russia did not have overseas colonies like many of the European countries. Instead, Russia seized neighboring territories. Its rulers expanded a small European state into a huge empire in Asia as well as in Europe. The czars controlled every aspect of the lives of the Russian people. For more than a hundred years after the revolutions that freed America from the British king and toppled the throne of France, the Romanovs ruled in Russia.

Czar Nicholas II and Czarina Alexandra with their children

Czar Alexander I (1801–1825) originally had some liberal ideas, but he never put into effect any of the social reforms he had discussed. Because he talked about making changes and nothing happened, he stirred up dissent among the people. When this happened he became a very harsh ruler.

Czar Nicholas I (1825–1855) learned a lesson from his brother's experience. He tolerated no liberal notions. His first act upon becoming czar was to hang the leaders of the Decembrist revolt, an uprising that lasted one day, December 14, 1825. He sent their followers into exile in Siberia. He was a cruel and brutal ruler who began the Crimean War in 1853 by invading Turkey. Russia was defeated when Britain and France came to Turkey's aid.

Czar Alexander II (1855–1881) had to begin his reign with the disaster left by his father: the aftermath of the Crimean War. He admired his uncle and wanted to put into effect some of the reforms his uncle had talked about. He freed the serfs in 1861 and tried other reforms. But he had the same results his uncle had: The more freedom he gave his people, the more they demanded. The freed serfs had no land and no way to make a living. Czar Alexander II reacted the same way his uncle had, too. He became a harsh and strict ruler. Of the many attempts to assassinate him, one finally succeeded. He was killed by a bomb while riding in his carriage.

Czar Alexander III (1881–1894) was near his father on the day of the assassination. He created a police force that brutally destroyed the terrorists and rooted out all liberal ideas. During the 1880s he succeeded in industrializing Russia. When he died in 1894, the basic social problems remained.

Czar Nicholas II (1894–1917) was the last of the Romanovs and the last czar of Russia. A weak and not very bright ruler, he withdrew into seclusion. During his reign the Trans-Siberian Railroad was built, and Russia joined the Allies during World War I. During the Russian revolution of 1917, he abdicated the throne. The Bolsheviks executed him and his family on July 16, 1918.

Mendeleyev wore his hair and beard long. Even though he
was one of Russia's leading intellectuals, he looked like a
Siberian peasant. He was very tall, with intense eyes,
and made up wild stories about his background, claiming
to be a pure Mongol from eastern Siberia.

2

The Young Scientist

Dmitri Ivanovich Mendeleyev was born in Tobolsk, Siberia, on February 7, 1834. He was the youngest of 14 children born to Ivan Pavlovitch Mendeleyev and Maria Dmitrievna Korniliev. He was a handsome, blue-eyed boy with blond hair. Nicknamed Mitia, he was his mother's favorite. When he was very young she began saving money for his education.

Shortly after Mitia was born, his father became blind. Ivan had to retire from the school he had directed. The small pension of a retired educator was not enough to support his large family. Maria became the main support of the family. She managed the glass factory the Korniliev family owned in the village of Aremziansk.

Maria had very progressive ideas. She built a new church for the workers and supervised the education of their children in the school she established. Not everyone appreciated her efforts. Some people said she was spoiling the workers. Others felt that by providing workers with some benefits, she was weakening the chances of a revolution that would overthrow the nobility.

The glass factory was young Mitia's favorite place. At the end of the school day he would race to the factory. From the chemist he learned about the elements that were mixed together to make the glass. From Timofei, the glass blower, he learned the art of shaping the melted glass into intricate and beautiful forms.

Mitia had a tutor, his sister Olga's husband, Bessargin. This man had been one of the Decembrists, a group of progressive nobles and intellectuals in St. Petersburg who wanted to see the end of serfdom. They also wanted a constitutional monarchy that would end the absolute power of the czars. When Alexander I died, they refused to swear allegiance to the new czar, Nicholas I. Along with members of the military who supported them, they staged an uprising on December 14, 1825. Their protest was crushed in a matter of hours. The ringleaders were immediately hanged and their followers, including Bessargin, were exiled to Siberia.

Bessargin married Mitia's older sister Olga. He was bored and restless in Siberia. He found few friends who were able to stimulate his active mind. He became interested in his intelligent young nephew. Mitia was an eager learner—as long as the subject was science. He had no interest in the classical education offered in his school.

From the three most important people in his life, Dmitri Mendeleyev was guided by three principles:

From his uncle and tutor Bessargin, "Everything in the world is science."

From the glass blower Timofei, "Everything in the world is art."

From his mother Maria, "Everything in the world is love."[1]

The boy understood that all three were true at the same time.

After two terrible years of tragedy, during which his father died of tuberculosis in 1847 and the glass factory burned in 1848, Mitia and his mother and sister made the long, hard journey to Moscow and St.

Petersburg in 1849. Mitia passed the entrance exams at the Pedagogical Institute, the school his father had attended. He did well enough to begin the science teacher training program with a full scholarship.

Shortly after Dmitri began his studies, his mother died. She was exhausted by her years of struggle and hard work. Then she'd made the long trip to St. Petersburg. At last she saw her beloved son enrolled in a program of higher education worthy of his abilities. She died of tuberculosis, the same terrible disease that had killed her husband. Less than a year later, Dmitri's sister Elizabeth also died of tuberculosis. Referring to himself in the third person, Mendeleyev eulogized his mother: "She instructed by example, corrected with love, and in order to devote him to science she left Siberia with him, spending thus her last resources and strength." [2]

Years later Mendeleyev dedicated a book to his mother. In the dedication he reported that her dying words to him had been, "Refrain from illusions, insist on work and not on words. Patiently search divine and scientific truth." [3]

Although the Pedagogical Institute was a teachers college, it had excellent science professors. It shared the buildings of St. Petersburg University, the finest academic institution in Russia. The science professors from the university taught the institute classes as well. Brilliant scientists headed both the physics and the chemistry departments. Dmitri Mendeleyev worked hard. He was soon at the head of his class. During his third year of studies he became very ill. The doctors told him that he had tuberculosis and would die within a few months.

His professors and classmates did everything they could to help him. His friends brought him his assignments. His teachers allowed him to do the necessary lab work and then to do the reading and write his reports in bed. Even though he was growing weaker, he was able to write original scientific papers that were published. In 1855, at the age of 21,

A huge crowd gathered in front of the University of St. Petersburg in 1917 to hear the Imperial Manifesto. Years earlier, in 1890, Dmitri Mendeleyev had been dismissed from this university for helping students who were protesting against unjust conditions.

he won the gold medal for best student of the year. He qualified as a teacher.

Despite his health, Mendeleyev took his first teaching assignment when he was assigned to Simferopol. It was the capital of Crimea, a peninsula thrusting into the Black Sea. The atmosphere on this beautiful southern coast was far different from the harsh climate of Siberia or St. Petersburg. The mild sunny weather and fresh sea air made it a place where many people went to recover their health. Dmitri Mendeleyev gradually grew stronger. He met a surgeon working at the local military hospital. This doctor examined him and found no trace of tuberculosis.

Eager to continue his scientific studies, Mendeleyev returned to St. Petersburg in 1856. He completed his master's thesis, "Expansion of Substances Due to Heat." This subject had fascinated him ever since his boyhood days at the glass factory. His instructors were so impressed that he was given a position lecturing about chemistry.

Czar Alexander II ruled Russia from 1855 to 1881. In the beginning of his reign he attempted many social reforms. He freed the serfs and improved the quality of education in Russia. As part of this effort the government paid for a young science teacher, Dmitri Mendeleyev, to study for two years in Europe with the major scientists of the time.

His teaching position was not paid. He depended on fees from his students. Dmitri didn't mind having very little money. He was used to that. What he did mind was that he had no opportunity to do advanced scientific research. Even though St. Petersburg had the best university in Russia, it was far behind the rest of Europe. Mendeleyev was frustrated.

He was 22 years old. From his mother, who had sacrificed everything to give him the opportunity, he had learned progressive ideas. From his tutor, Bessargin, he had learned that others had made great sacrifices for social change. He loved his country and felt that he could best achieve social progress by the practical application of science.

In Russian history, the years between about 1855 and 1865 are known as the Great Reform Era. Czar Nicholas I, who reigned between 1825 and 1855, was a brutal tyrant. Anyone who opposed him was jailed, sent to Siberian prison camps, or exiled. The czar's police watched the universities closely for any sign of dissenting opinions.

When Nicholas died in 1855, his son, Alexander II, realized that reforms were necessary. He understood that revolutions, like the one that had toppled the monarchy in France, occurred when the people had no hope of change. He also realized that the quality of education had to be improved, that Russia needed more educated citizens.

Everyone who could pass the entrance exams was admitted to the universities. The number of students increased rapidly. Scholarly material that had been forbidden was allowed into the country. Subjects that had been illegal to teach were introduced into the curriculum. The emphasis that the new czar was putting on education made the students feel important. Many of them came from the lower classes. For the first time the young members of the aristocracy had classmates coming from backgrounds of poverty.

Caught up in the currents of history, Dmitri Mendeleyev faced the eager young students in his classes. He was determined to teach them everything he knew. But he knew that he didn't know enough. He had a great deal to learn that he could not learn in Russia.

Peter the Great, the powerful czar who dragged and bullied his enormous country into the world of 18th-century Europe, built his city, St. Petersburg, on the banks of the Neva River where it flowed into the Gulf of Finland, which opened onto the Baltic Sea. Peter hated and feared Moscow, the former capital city. His boyhood in the capital had been terrorized with violent attempts on his life. He never felt safe there.

Church of the Savior on Spilled Blood, St. Petersburg, Russia

In addition to his hatred of Moscow, Peter needed a capital that would be a seaport. He had studied shipbuilding in Amsterdam. He wanted a port city where ships from all the countries of Europe could bring ideas and goods from the west—and where the Russian fleet that he would build could set sail for European ports. St. Petersburg was built to be Russia's open window to the west. Architects from France, sculptors from Italy, craftsmen from Germany, and artists and musicians from all over Europe were invited to Peter's court to help build his beautiful city.

But the swamps had to be drained before the building could begin. A system of canals channeled the water. Dirt was hauled long distances, sometimes in carts, sometimes on the backs of peasants, to provide the landfill that would be a foundation for building. St. Petersburg was built on swampland, and on the bones of thousands of Russian peasants who died from the hard labor and unhealthy conditions of the mosquito-infested swamps.

Once the site was ready, the nobility began to build their magnificent palaces on the embankments of the canals and of the Neva. Chief among all of the brilliant examples of baroque and neoclassical architecture of the 18th and 19th centuries is the Winter Palace, residence of the czars. It now is part of the Hermitage, one of the major art museums of the world. Peter the Great passed a law decreeing that no building in St. Petersburg should be higher than the Winter Palace. As a result, St. Petersburg is a spacious city open to the sky, its wide streets and lovely vistas free of the towering skyscrapers that dominate most modern cities. It is a center of art and culture unsurpassed by any other city in the world.

This portrait of Dmitri Mendeleyev by an unknown artist shows him writing in his laboratory. Mendeleyev's book on organic chemistry won the Domidov Prize in 1861. He began his masterwork, *The Principles of Chemistry*, in 1867. His efforts to organize this book led to his discovery of the Periodic Table of Elements.

3

Siberian Wild Man

Russian universities were not as advanced in scientific studies as the schools in Western Europe. By 1859 the Russian government had begun to modernize its educational system. As part of this effort, they paid for the promising young science teacher, Dmitri Mendeleyev, to study for two years in Europe. His task was to bring home new scientific ideas.

Mendeleyev traveled first to Paris. He studied with Henri Regnault, a very good experimental scientist who worked with gases. Next he went to Heidelberg where Gustav Kirchhoff and Robert Bunsen were developing the spectroscope. They found that when an element was heated, the light it emitted had its own spectrum of colored lines. This research was greatly helped by the Bunsen burner, which provided a flame that had almost no background light. Shortly before Mendeleyev's arrival in Germany, Kirchhoff and Bunsen had discovered a new element that produced deep red lines in its spectrum. They named the new element rubidium because of the ruby red lines.

These were exciting times for the science of chemistry. Dmitri Mendeleyev was right in the middle of amazing discoveries. When Kirchhoff studied sunlight with the spectroscope, he discovered new elements in the sun that had not been found on Earth. Working in

Bunsen's laboratory, Mendeleyev gained greatly in his knowledge of chemical elements.

Unfortunately, Dmitri's confidence in his own abilities, and his short temper, put an end to this arrangement. He did not get along with Bunsen. After a loud disagreement, Dmitri left the lab in a rage, swearing he would never return. In fact, he had made Bunsen so angry, he couldn't have returned even if he had wanted to. Dmitri made a small laboratory in his living quarters. He continued his researches on his own. He was, of course, limited to rather simple experiments. His experiments soon led him to investigate the nature of solutions, which in turn revealed much about atoms and molecules and their valences. (The valence of an atom is its ability to combine with other atoms.) Mendeleyev learned a lot while making what seemed like simple experiments with the solubility of alcohol in water.

Stubbornly working alone in his rooms in Heidelberg, Mendeleyev also discovered that every gas has a critical temperature. This means that when it is heated above that temperature, no amount of pressure can turn it into a liquid. Two years later Thomas Andrews, an Irish chemist, made the same discovery. He was given credit for the discovery because Mendeleyev's report had gone unnoticed.

In September 1860, the first international chemistry congress was held at Karlsruhe in Germany. Leading chemists from all over Europe attended, and so did young Dmitri Mendeleyev. He temporarily left his self-imposed isolation in nearby Heidelberg. The purpose of the gathering was to establish a common system for measuring the weights of the different elements. Without such a system to use as a standard, the body of scientific knowledge could not develop. Scientists could not learn from each other's experiments if they did not agree on how to measure the weights of elements.

They all agreed that the elements should be weighed relative to the lightest known element, which was hydrogen. But they didn't agree on how those relative weights should be made. Some chemists wanted to use the atomic weight system, while others wanted to use the equivalent weight system. These two systems provided different results. Chemical papers and reports were being published without any mention of which system was being used, which produced not only confusion but also dangerous situations in the laboratories.

The conference in Karlsruhe confirmed Mendeleyev's belief that it was the atomic weight of an atom that mattered. No hope of discovering a way to organize the elements into a clear pattern could exist without such a basic agreement.

In 1861 Dmitri Mendeleyev returned to Russia to teach at the Technical Institute in St. Petersburg. He found that none of the exciting new developments in chemistry had reached Russia. Dmitri was only 27 years old, but he already had a flowing beard and wild unruly long hair—and he only trimmed them once a year. One observer noted, "Every hair acted separate from the others."[1] A very tall man with intense blue eyes, Mendeleyev looked like a cross between a Siberian bear and a mad prophet. He enjoyed making up wild tales about his Siberian background, claiming that he was a pure Mongol from eastern Siberia and had not even learned how to speak Russian until he was 17 years old. In fact he was actually a kind of prophet, lecturing enthusiastically about the latest developments in chemistry. When he found that there was no existing textbook on modern organic chemistry, he wrote one. His text was awarded the Domidov Prize. He was gaining quite a reputation.

An even more significant event in 1861 was the liberation of the serfs by Alexander II. At the czar's decree, millions of Russians were no longer property and part of their masters' possessions. Social and economic conditions were in chaos. The value of land dropped drastically. When Dmitri Mendeleyev became a full professor in 1864, he was able to lease a small estate at Tver, southeast of St. Petersburg. He introduced scientific farming methods to the peasants. These methods attracted attention. Soon the authorities began seeking Mendeleyev's advice on many practical applications of science.

Meanwhile, back in Siberia, Dmitri's family was following his career with pride. His sister Olga thought that so successful a man should have a wife. She busied herself finding one for him. The Siberian woman his sister chose was Feozva Nikitchna Lascheva. She and Dmitri were married in 1863, but they didn't get along. She asked him once whether he was married to her or to science. He replied that he "was married to both of them unless that was bigamy, in which case he was married to science."[2]

In spite of their differences, they had a son named Vladimir and a daughter named Olga. Feozva managed their domestic life by living on the estate at Tver while Dmitri was in St. Petersburg at the university. She went to their home in St. Petersburg while he was at the estate in Tver. The marriage thus worked fairly well for 19 years.

Mendeleyev's love of science, and of its practical applications, made him a popular teacher. One of his students, the future anarchist Pyotr Kropotkin, remembered:

> The hall was always crowded with something like two hundred
> students, many of whom, I am afraid, could not follow
> Mendeleyev, but for the few of us who could it was a stimulant
> to the intellect and a lesson in scientific thinking which must
> have left deep traces in their development, as it did in mine.[3]

Mendeleyev taught not only students, but also anyone else who would listen to him. When he traveled, he went third-class with the *mouzhiks,* the Russian peasants. With his rough, wild appearance he looked like one of them. They would gather around him as he talked of ways they could improve the yield of their crops or their methods for making cheese. The peasants desperately needed help. Although they were free, all too often this meant that they were free to starve. Powerful members of the aristocracy no longer owned them, but they themselves owned nothing. The land available was owned by communes, not by individual peasants.

The Russian peasants were poor, uneducated, and illiterate, but hardworking and eager to learn. Mendeleyev loved his countrymen. They came to him for advice and he helped them learn better farming methods. He knew that their very survival depended upon applying the principles of science to their labors. The government realized the value of Mendeleyev's efforts and sent him traveling the length and breadth of his huge country to develop its resources.

Manifesto

The Communist Manifesto was first published in 1848. A manifesto is a document that proclaims—makes manifest—the ideas of a group or individual. In this case the writers were two individuals, Karl Marx and Friedrich Engels. Marx was born in Prussia in 1818 and was educated there. He believed that economics rather than philosophy created social reality.

Karl Marx

After earning a doctorate in 1841, Marx tried to get jobs as a journalist in Paris and Brussels. His unpopular political ideas made it difficult for him to earn a living. Marx and his colleague Engels issued The Communist Manifesto in hopes of causing social change. At first their manifesto had little influence. Not until other writings by Marx and Engels made their views widely known did it become important.

In their manifesto, Marx and Engels claimed that all of human history was a history of class struggle. They believed that the industrial societies of the 19th century had simplified the class struggle by splitting society into two groups: the bourgeoisie (the wealthy owners of the factories and means of production) and the proletariat (the workers whose labor was exploited for the profit of the wealthy owners).

Although the organization for which the manifesto was written was illegal, Marx believed that eventually the socialist movement would be open. He thought that once the workers understood how they were enslaved and the benefits of their labor taken from them, revolution would naturally follow.

He thought that communism would be developed in stages: First there would be socialism, which is government ownership of means of production. Then the government control would wither away and the workers would work for the common good, "from each according to his ability, to each according to his needs." Once the workers from all over the world had taken control and national boundaries and governments had disappeared, there would be no more war and no more poverty.

Friedrich Engels

Radical ideas like those of Marx and Engels swept through Europe. In Russia they became the foundation of the revolution that overthrew the last of the czars and established the Soviet Union in the early years of the 20th century.

In addition to being a brilliant scientist, Dmitri Mendeleyev was an inspired teacher. Hundreds of students crowded his lectures at the University of St. Petersburg. He traveled the length and breadth of his huge country to teach the peasants better farming methods and to help industries such as the Russian oil producers develop better production methods.

Scientific Advancements of the 19th Century

4

Periodic Patience

Mendeleyev was painfully aware that many of his students "could not follow" him, as Kropotkin had observed. A large part of the problem was the lack of any clear system for organizing the known elements. Without such a system, he could only present details about the properties of various elements. He could not present the framework that would give meaning to the details. As he put it:

> The edifice of science requires not only material, but also a plan,
> and necessitates the work of preparing the materials, putting them
> together, working out the plans and symmetrical proportions of the
> various parts.[1]

His lectures were on inorganic chemistry, the study of the basic chemical elements. Once again he found that there was no good textbook available in Russian. He had written the only textbook for organic chemistry, and now he sat down to write a text for inorganic chemistry. The result would be *The Principles of Chemistry*. It would be translated into all the major languages of the world. It would remain the standard work in the field of chemistry until early in the 20th century.

Mendeleyev began writing his masterwork in 1867. The first volume went smoothly enough. It included what he called "typical"[2] elements:

29

hydrogen, oxygen, nitrogen, and carbon. The valences of these elements provided a natural order of presentation. Next he included the halogens, five elements that react easily with other elements. All of these elements had low atomic weights and were widely available in nature. He had begun by using atomic weights as a method of organization. But then he was stuck.

At that time there were 63 known elements. He wrote the atomic weight and the properties of each element on a card. He took the cards with him everywhere he went, playing what he called "chemical solitaire" with them when he went on long train trips. He must have looked like some mysterious Siberian shaman, this enormous bearlike man laying out cards with strange symbols on them. He seemed to be playing an odd game of patience, the solitaire game in which playing cards are arranged in rows.

By February 1869 he realized that "elements placed according to the value of their atomic weights present a clear periodicity of properties."[3] But exactly what was this periodicity?

On Monday, February 17, Mendeleyev was supposed to travel to Tver to meet with cheese makers of the Voluntary Economic Cooperative. In the morning mail he received a letter giving the details of the meeting and for the tour of the province's cheese-making centers. He was supposed to catch the train right after breakfast. He took the letter and his tea to his desk and began scribbling notes on the back of the letter, listing some elements and their atomic weights. (The letter, with its ring where he had set his teacup, is still in existence.)[4]

He had been working on this problem of organizing the elements for three days and nights. He had taken his cards with the elements on them and tacked them on the wall of his study. He arranged them and rearranged them. Nothing worked. The train was forgotten. A friend who visited him in the afternoon found him frustrated. "It's all formed in my head," he said, "but I can't express it."[5] He was sure that somehow the cards could be organized as they are in the game of patience: The atomic weights of the elements would represent the numerical order of the cards; their similar properties would be like the suits of cards. But he couldn't get them to fit together. Exhausted from days of effort with very little sleep, he rested his head on his arms and fell asleep.

Later he said, "I saw in a dream a table where all the elements fell into place as required. Awakening, I immediately wrote it down on a piece of paper."[6] He named his discovery the Periodic Table of the Elements. With some revisions, this is the table that can be found to this day hanging on the wall of every chemistry classroom in the world.

Mendeleyev first drew the periodic table after his dream in which his mind had continued to work on the problem even though he was asleep. However, there were still some places where the pattern wasn't clear. For example, in some cases where the elements were grouped according to their properties, the order of the atomic weights was incorrect. With his usual self-confidence, Mendeleyev decided that the atomic weights were wrong, not his system. Where there was a gap in the order, he predicted that there was an element that belonged there, but it had not been discovered yet. He even gave names and descriptions and atomic weights to the missing elements!

Two weeks later when he published his paper, "A Suggested System of the Elements," many other scientists were not convinced. There were just too many inconsistencies, too many holes, and too many places where the atomic weights didn't follow the pattern. They laughed at the notion of a scientific theory that claimed scientific errors for its support. For example, Mendeleyev had put platinum, which had an atomic weight of 196.7, in the position that gold should have had. Critics were quick to point out the supposed error, because gold was thought to have an atomic weight of 196.2. But Mendeleyev was right. When it was reexamined, the atomic weight of gold was found to be greater than that of platinum.

As often happens in the development of science, another man arrived at the same theory at the same time. German scientist Julius

Lothar Meyer published a paper in 1870 describing the same organization of elements as Mendeleyev had produced. Meyer and Mendeleyev had very similar backgrounds: Both had studied at Heidelberg in Bunsen's laboratory (although Meyer did not leave in a rage); both had attended the conference in Karlsruhe; and both were teachers working on textbooks for their students.

It is perhaps not fair that Mendeleyev received all the credit for the periodic table while Meyer remained unknown. The reason for this is to be found in the difference in the personalities of the two men as much as in the fact that Mendeleyev published his findings before Meyer published his. Meyer was cautious in stating his theory. Mendeleyev was boldly confident that his theory was correct.

Even more dramatic than the revisions of atomic weights were the discoveries of elements that Mendeleyev predicted would be found to fit into the gaps in his table. In 1875 a French chemist, Paul "Francois" Lecoq de Boisbaudran, discovered gallium, an element that exactly matched Mendeleyev's description and atomic weight for what he called "eka-aluminum."[7] But when Lecoq calculated the specific gravity of the new element, he found that it was 4.7. Mendeleyev had predicted that his eka-aluminum would have a specific gravity of 5.9. This was a serious anomaly.

When Mendeleyev heard that Lecoq's findings did not match his prediction, he did not doubt his own work. He immediately wrote to Lecoq and told him to do the experiments again with a pure sample of the new element. Lecoq followed instructions. Using a larger sample, he found that the specific gravity of gallium was indeed 5.9, just as Mendeleyev had predicted.

In 1886 a German chemist found germanium, another element that Mendeleyev had predicted. The scientific world was both astonished and totally convinced: Mendeleyev had succeeded in discovering the order of the elements.

The ancient Greeks tried to figure out what the world was made of. Even though many of their theories were later disproved, their efforts to observe and make experiments were the foundation of science. Around 400 B.C., Democritus proposed the idea that everything in the world was made up of tiny particles, which he called "atoms" from the Greek word meaning "unable to be cut." He thought that these little building blocks of matter were the smallest possible units, and that they made up everything in the universe. This theory was partly wrong and partly right.

A computer-generated image of an atom

The part that was wrong was that atoms are the smallest possible things. Scientists now know that atoms are made up of even smaller parts: A neutron is part of the nucleus, or central part, of an atom. It has no electrical charge and so is neutral. A proton is the other part of the nucleus; it has a positive charge. Electrons are very, very small particles that have a negative charge. They orbit the nucleus like the planets in a tiny solar system.

The part of the Greek theory that was right was that atoms are the smallest parts of an element that still have all the characteristics of that element. In the 18th and 19th centuries, chemists began a serious search to find how many elements—that is, how many different kinds of atoms—exist. And as they isolated different elements, they needed a way to organize and understand these basic units that make up the entire universe.

At the beginning of the 19th century, an English teacher and scientist named John Dalton made these statements about atoms: 1) All atoms of any element are the same. 2) Atoms of different elements are different in size and properties. 3) Atoms of different elements can combine to form compounds. 4) In these compounds the atoms are not changed, and the numbers and kinds remain the same. Dalton's theory became the basis for modern chemistry.

Since all atoms of any element are alike, and not like the atoms of any other element, one way to tell them apart would be to weigh them. Of course atoms are too small to put on a scale, so other chemists figured out how to determine their relative weights.

They used hydrogen, the lightest element for their standard. They found that a liter of oxygen weighted 16 times as much as a liter of hydrogen, so they gave oxygen an atomic weight of 16. By finding the atomic weights of each element they discovered, chemists had the beginning of a way to organize the elements.

Mendeleyev was a social visionary as well as a scientific genius. His love of his country and his people, the Russian peasants, caused him to work tirelessly to improve farming methods so that the recently freed serfs could make a living. He also encouraged his students in their protests against injustice.

5

Love of Country

Mendeleyev's Periodic Table of the Elements is the basis of modern chemistry. It has been used to predict the possible combinations of atoms into molecules. This has led to remarkable chemical discoveries, from plastics and synthetic fibers to miracle drugs and the complex DNA molecule—the basic building block of life. The scientific advances of well over a century rest on Mendeleyev's discovery. The periodic table has had adjustments and rearrangements as it expanded to include nearly double the number of elements with which it was originally organized. But the basic structure remains the same. The properties, valences, and weights of the elements are now known to depend on particles within the atoms. Modern nuclear physics has demonstrated through experiments that Mendeleyev's idea was correct.

For most of the world, Mendeleyev's fame rests on the Periodic Table of Elements. In Russia this great scientist is remembered for many other achievements as well. As his country's primary scientific adviser, he was constantly traveling and working to modernize both agriculture and industry. He loved the Russian people. After the serfs were freed in 1861, he realized that Russia would have to develop efficient methods of production to provide the people with the opportunity to make a living.

In the United States, oil had been discovered in Pennsylvania in 1859. American oil products were being sent all over the world, including to Russia. Mendeleyev criticized his government for being slow in developing the oil fields near Baku on the Caspian Sea. He wanted to open the oil industry to foreign investors. In 1876 he traveled to America as consultant for Russian oil producers.

Mendeleyev did not like America, although he found the development of the Pennsylvania oil fields interesting. Probably he had visions of the United States as a promised land of freedom and democracy where all social problems had been solved. Instead he found a raw young country not yet recovered from the bitterness of civil war. He complained about the Americans:

> Why do they hate Negroes, Indians, even Germans? . . Why are
> there so many frauds and so much nonsense? . . . It was clear that
> in the United States there was a development not of the best, but
> of the middle and worst sides of European civilization.[1]

New York, with its narrow crowded streets and tall buildings, did not impress him. He compared it to the spacious avenues and beautiful architecture of St. Petersburg. And it was far too hot in the summer for a Siberian. Mendeleyev went home early.

Also in 1876, when he was 42 years old, Mendeleyev fell in love. The young woman was a 17-year-old art student, the best friend of one of his nieces. Dmitri followed the girl to Rome, then returned to Russia determined to marry her. He convinced his wife, Feozva, to grant him a divorce. It became final in January of 1882. According to the Russian Orthodox Church, it was necessary to wait seven years after a divorce before marrying a second time. Mendeleyev threatened to drown himself if he could not marry immediately. He found a priest who married him to Anna Ivanova Popova. This caused a great scandal. The priest was removed from the priesthood. Members of the nobility at court complained to Czar Alexander III that Mendeleyev was a bigamist. The czar shrugged. "I admit Mendeleyev has two wives," he said, "but I have only one Mendeleyev."[2]

Dmitri and Anna had a very happy marriage and were together until Mendeleyev's death. They had four children, Liubov, Ivan, and twins Vassili and Maria. Anna inspired an interest in art in Dmitri. He was elected to the Academy of Arts for his painting and his art criticism. (Oddly enough he was never elected to the Academy of Sciences.)

Throughout his life Dmitri Mendeleyev witnessed the sufferings of his people. The cruel oppression of the Romanov czars and the Russian nobility forced the peasants to live lives of poverty and hard labor. As a child Dmitri saw the efforts his mother made to provide education for the workers in the glass factory in the village of Aremziansk. His tutor, Bessargin, told him about the radical ideas that were sweeping Europe.

Mendeleyev believed that the best way to help his people was through science. In 1890, however, he assisted the students at the University of St. Petersburg who were protesting against unjust conditions. He agreed to take their petition to the administration. The minister of education was outraged. He dismissed Mendeleyev from his position at the university, saying that he "should have stuck to teaching and forgotten about politics."[3]

The state police interrupted Mendeleyev's last lecture at the university. The authorities were afraid he would lead a student uprising. In his lecture he told his students:

> I have achieved an inner freedom. There is nothing in this world
> that I fear to say. No one nor anything can silence me. This is a
> good feeling. This is the feeling of a man. I want you to have this
> feeling too—it is my moral responsibility to help you achieve this
> inner freedom. I am an evolutionist of a peaceable type. Proceed in
> a logical and systematic manner. [4]

Two years after he was dismissed from the university, the Russian government asked Mendeleyev to become head of their Bureau of

Periodic Table of the Elements

Group**

Period	1 IA 1A																		18 vIIIA 8A

	1	2											13	14	15	16	17	2
1	**H** IIA 1.008 2A												IIIA IVA VA VIA VIIA 3A 4A 5A 6A 7A					**He** 4.003

| 2 | 3 **Li** 6.941 | 4 **Be** 9.012 | | | | | | | | | | | 5 **B** 10.81 | 6 **C** 12.01 | 7 **N** 14.01 | 8 **O** 16.00 | 9 **F** 19.00 | 10 **Ne** 20.18 |

| 3 | 11 **Na** 22.99 | 12 **Mg** 24.31 | 3 IIIB 3B | 4 IVB 4B | 5 VB 5B | 6 VIB 6B | 7 VIIB 7B | 8 ------- VIII ------- 8 ------- | 9 | 10 | 11 IB 1B | 12 IIB 2B | 13 **Al** 26.98 | 14 **Si** 28.09 | 15 **P** 30.97 | 16 **S** 32.07 | 17 **Cl** 35.45 | 18 **Ar** 39.95 |

| 4 | 19 **K** 39.10 | 20 **Ca** 40.08 | 21 **Sc** 44.96 | 22 **Ti** 47.88 | 23 **V** 50.94 | 24 **Cr** 52.00 | 25 **Mn** 54.94 | 26 **Fe** 55.85 | 27 **Co** 58.47 | 28 **Ni** 58.69 | 29 **Cu** 63.55 | 30 **Zn** 65.39 | 31 **Ga** 69.72 | 32 **Ge** 72.59 | 33 **As** 74.92 | 34 **Se** 78.96 | 35 **Br** 79.90 | 36 **Kr** 83.80 |

| 5 | 37 **Rb** 85.47 | 38 **Sr** 87.62 | 39 **Y** 88.91 | 40 **Zr** 91.22 | 41 **Nb** 92.91 | 42 **Mo** 95.94 | 43 **Tc** (98) | 44 **Ru** 101.1 | 45 **Rh** 102.9 | 46 **Pd** 106.4 | 47 **Ag** 107.9 | 48 **Cd** 112.4 | 49 **In** 114.8 | 50 **Sn** 118.7 | 51 **Sb** 121.8 | 52 **Te** 127.6 | 53 **I** 126.9 | 54 **Xe** 131.3 |

| 6 | 55 **Cs** 132.9 | 56 **Ba** 137.3 | 57 **La*** 138.9 | 72 **Hf** 178.5 | 73 **Ta** 180.9 | 74 **W** 183.9 | 75 **Re** 186.2 | 76 **Os** 190.2 | 77 **Ir** 190.2 | 78 **Pt** 195.1 | 79 **Au** 197.0 | 80 **Hg** 200.5 | 81 **Tl** 204.4 | 82 **Pb** 207.2 | 83 **Bi** 209.0 | 84 **Po** (210) | 85 **At** (210) | 86 **Rn** (222) |

| 7 | 87 **Fr** (223) | 88 **Ra** (226) | 89 **Ac~** (227) | 104 **Rf** (257) | 105 **Db** (260) | 106 **Sg** (263) | 107 **Bh** (262) | 108 **Hs** (265) | 109 **Mt** (266) | 110 --- 0 | 111 --- 0 | 112 --- 0 | 114 --- 0 | | 116 --- 0 | | 118 --- 0 |

Lanthanide Series*

58 **Ce** 140.1	59 **Pr** 140.9	60 **Nd** 144.2	61 **Pm** (147)	62 **Sm** 150.4	63 **Eu** 152.0	64 **Gd** 157.3	65 **Tb** 158.9	66 **Dy** 162.5	67 **Ho** 164.9	68 **Er** 167.3	69 **Tm** 168.9	70 **Yb** 173.0	71 **Lu** 175.0

Actinide Series~

90 **Th** 232.0	91 **Pa** (231)	92 **U** (238)	93 **Np** (237)	94 **Pu** (242)	95 **Am** (243)	96 **Cm** (247)	97 **Bk** (247)	98 **Cf** (249)	99 **Es** (254)	100 **Fm** (253)	101 **Md** (256)	102 **No** (254)	103 **Lr** (257)

Mendeleyev's understanding that chemical science could not develop further without an organizing principle led to his discovery of the Periodic Table of Elements. His work, at first doubted by other scientists, is the basis of modern chemistry. The modern Periodic Table is based on Mendeleyev's work and is displayed in science classrooms and labratories around the world.

Weights and Measures. Many people thought that this position was offered to him to quiet the unrest following the loss of his teaching position. Whatever the reason, he made many important contributions to the problems of establishing standard measures. He continued in this post until his death and remained one of the most popular figures in Russia. He also received many awards from scientific organizations throughout the world. The Royal Society of England awarded him the Copley Medal, its highest award, in 1905. Universities around the world gave Mendeleyev honorary degrees.

He died of influenza in 1907 at the age of 73. Students from the university carried large models of his periodic table in the funeral procession through the streets of St. Petersburg. He was buried beside his mother.

A lot still remained to be learned about Mendeleyev's legacy to the world, his Periodic Table of Elements. For example, although it demonstrated that the properties of elements recurred periodically, it didn't explain why. In 1913 a British physicist, Henry Moseley, experimented with X-ray diffraction. He found that it was the nuclear charge—that is, the number of protons in the nucleus, called the atomic number—that determined an element's place in the periodic table. Because the atomic weight is determined primarily by the weight of the protons, Mendeleyev's organization was correct even though he was not entirely correct about the reasons behind the organization.

New elements continued to be discovered throughout the 20th century. Three new elements, numbers 116, 117, and 118, were identified in 1999 alone. Scientists name new elements for countries (like germanium and americium), or for states (californium), and even for universities (berkelium). Usually, however, the names of newly discovered elements are taken from the names of famous scientists: einsteinium from Albert Einstein, curium from Marie Curie, and fermium from Enrico Fermi. In 1955 scientists identified element 101, which they called mendelevium.

Mendeleyev's remarkable achievement is that even though it is greatly expanded to include dozens of elements discovered since his death, his Periodic Table of the Elements has remained the most accurate method of classifying the tiny building blocks of the universe, the atoms.

Present-day Russia, shown in this map, is very different from Imperial Russia of the 19th Century. Tobolsk, where Mendeleyev was born, is in eastern Siberia. The Ukraine, where young Dmitri Mendeleyev taught, was at that time part of Russia. Even though the maps have changed, this map shows the enormous distances Mendeleyev traveled to help his people develop better production methods.

Industry

The petroleum industry was born only around 150 years ago. This enormous and powerful industry now controls the fate of nations. For thousands of years, however, people had very little use for oil. In the 1750s American colonists digging for salt found oil instead—and considered it a nuisance. Not until the

Oil rig in the sea

1840s, when a Canadian geologist discovered kerosene, which could be distilled from oil, did oil rise in value.

The oil industry began on a large scale in 1859. A retired railroad conductor named Edwin Drake drilled a well near Titusville, Pennsylvania. He used an old steam engine to power the drill. When his well began to produce oil, other prospectors drilled wells in the area. By the 1860s oil derricks covered the hills. The oil rush in Pennsylvania was like the gold rush in California had been 10 years earlier.

Oil production spread quickly to other parts of the United States and to other countries of the world. In Russia oil wells near Baku on the Caspian Sea began to produce. A pipeline through the mountains east of Baku led to the first organized shipping enterprise to compete with the U.S. and send kerosene to Europe. Not until the beginning of the 20th century were important oil discoveries made in Iran, Iraq, Saudi Arabia, and other countries on the Persian Gulf.

In the beginning, kerosene for lamps and stoves was the main product of the petroleum industry. Refiners thought gasoline was a useless by-product and dumped it. Then at the beginning of the 20th century, two developments changed the industry: The electric light replaced kerosene lamps, and the automobile replaced the horse. The market for kerosene nearly disappeared just as the demand for gasoline became enormous.

At first the refineries were not efficient. It took 100 barrels of crude oil to produce about 11 barrels of gasoline. A new process developed in 1913 doubled the amount of gasoline produced from a barrel of oil. World War I (1914–1918) created a huge demand for petroleum fuels for ships and airplanes. Fuel became as important as ammunition in fighting a war. The increasing demand for oil products has not only continued but has increased until the present day—and shows no sign of slowing down.

Chronology

1834	Born in Tobolsk, Siberia, a province of Russia, on February 7
1847	Father, Ivan Pavlovich Mendeleyev, dies of tuberculosis
1848	Glass factory where his mother was manager burns
1849	Travels with mother and sister in wagon from Tobolsk to Moscow and St. Petersburg
1850	Enrolls in Pedagogical Institute in St. Petersburg; mother, Maria Dmitrievna Korniliev, and sister Elizabeth die of tuberculosis
1855	Graduates as science teacher and accepts post in Simferopol in the Crimea
1856	Returns to St. Petersburg to defend his master's thesis and lecture in chemistry
1859	Minister of Public Instruction assigns him to study abroad; studies with Regnault in Paris and Kirchhoff and Bunsen in Heidelberg
1860	Attends Chemical Congress at Karlsruhe discussing atomic weights
1861	Returns to St. Petersburg; publishes textbook, *Organic Chemistry*, which won the Domidov Prize
1863	Becomes professor of chemistry at the Technological Institute; marries Feozva Nikitchna Lascheva
1866	Becomes professor of chemistry at University of St. Petersburg and is made doctor of science for his dissertation
1868	Helps to found the Russian Chemical Society; publishes first edition of *Principles of Chemistry*
1869	Creates the Periodic Table of the Elements
1876	Visits the United States to see the Pennsylvania oil fields
1882	Divorces his first wife and marries young art student, Anna Ivanova Popova
1887	Makes solo ascent in a balloon to observe solar eclipse
1890	Is dismissed from university teaching position for supporting student dissent
1893	Accepts post as Director of Bureau of Weights and Measures
1905	Royal Society of England awards him their highest award, the Copley Medal
1907	Dies of influenza in St. Petersburg on January 20

Timeline in Chemistry

c. 400 B.C.	Greek philosopher Democritus names the tiniest particles of matter *atomos,* "that which cannot be split."
1787	Jacques Charles formulates Charles's law, which relates volume changes of gases with changes in temperature.
1789	Antoine-Laurent Lavoisier publishes *Elements of Chemistry.*
1811	Amedeo Avogadro demonstrates that equal volumes of all gases under the same temperature and pressure contain the same number of molecules.
1828	Friedrich Wöhler synthesizes the first organic compound from inorganic compounds.
1835	Jöns Berzelius publishes the first general theory of chemical catalysis.
1845	Adolf Wilhelm Hermann Kolbe synthesizes acetic acid.
1859	Robert Bunsen and Gustav Kirchhoff develop spectroscope, which they are using when they discover two elements, cesium (1860) and rubidium (1861).
1869	Dmitri Mendeleyev publishes his Periodic Table of the Elements.
1876	The American Chemical Society (ACS) is formed.
1878	Josiah Gibbs develops the theory of chemical thermodynamics.
1884	S. A. Arrhenius and F. W. Ostwald independently define acids as substances that release hydrogen ions when dissolved in water.
1887	Emil Fischer elaborates the structural patterns of proteins.
1895	Carl Linde develops a process for liquefying air.
1898	Marie Curie discovers radium.
1903	Arthur Noyes, MIT professor, establishes Research Laboratory of Physical Chemistry.
1913	Henry Moseley uses X-ray diffraction to establish the significance of atomic number.
1939	Linus Pauling publishes *The Nature of the Chemical Bond.*
1941	American chemists Glenn Seaborg, Edwin McMillan, Joseph Kennedy, and Arthur Wahl create the first human-made element, plutonium.
1953	Francis Crick and James Watson solve double-helix structure of DNA.
1981	Chemical process simulation software is released for PCs; Gerd Binnig and Heinrich Rohrer develop scanning tunneling microscope, which can resolve individual atoms on a surface.
1999	Three new human-made elements—116, 117, and 118—are created.
2000	Human genome project completed, showing that humans possess around 30,000 genes.
2003	Smithsonian Institution opens exhibit of human genome project to celebrate 50th anniversary of solving the double-helix structure of DNA.
2004	Scientists create and add elements 113 and 115 to the Periodic Table.

Chapter Notes

Chapter 1   **Fire!**

  1. Leslie Alan Horvitz, *Eureka! Scientific Breakthroughs that Changed the World,* (New York: John Wiley & Sons, Inc., 2002), p.46.

Chapter 2   **The Young Scientist**

  1. Woodrow Wilson Leadership Program in Chemistry: Dmitri Ivanovich Mendeleev http://www.woodrow.org/teachers/ci/1992/Mendeleev.html p.1.
  2. ibid.
  3. Paul Strathern, *Mendeleyev's Dream: The Quest for the Elements.* (New York: St. Martin's Press, 2000), p. 264.

Chapter 3   **Siberian Wild Man**

  1.Leslie Alan Horvitz, *Eureka! Scientific Breakthroughs that Changed the World.* (New York: John Wiley & Sons, Inc., 2002), p.45.
  2.Woodrow Wilson Leadership Program in Chemistry: Dmitri Ivanovich Mendeleev http://www.woodrow.org/teachers/ci/1992/Mendeleev.html p. 4.
  3. Paul Strathern, *Mendeleyev's Dream: The Quest for the Elements,* (New York: St. Martin's Press, 2000), p. 276.

Chapter 4   **Periodic Patience**

  1. Paul Strathern, *Mendeleyev's Dream: The Quest for the Elements,* (New York: St. Martin's Press, 2000), p. 277.
  2. William Brock *The Chemical Tree: A History of Chemistry,* (New York: W.W. Norton & Company, 1992), p. 319.
  3. ibid. p. 320.
  4. Paul Strathern, *Mendeleyev's Dream: The Quest for the Elements,* (New York: St. Martin's Press, 2000), p. 281.
  5. ibid. p. 283.
  6. ibid. p. 286.
  7. Leslie Alan Horvitz, *Eureka! Scientific Breakthroughs that Changed the World.* (New York: John Wiley & Sons, Inc., 2002), p. 53.

Chapter 5   **Love of Country**

  1. William Brock *The Chemical Tree: A History of Chemistry,* (New York: W.W. Norton & Company, 1992), p. 351.
  2. ibid. p. 351.
  3. Leslie Alan Horvitz, *Eureka! Scientific Breakthroughs that Changed the World.* (New York: John Wiley & Sons, Inc., 2002), p. 54.
  4. Woodrow Wilson Leadership Program in Chemistry: Dmitri Ivanovich Mendeleyev http://www.woodrow.org/teachers/ci/1992/Mendeleev.html p. 6.

Glossary

abdicate (AB-duh-kayt) to give up a throne.

baroque (buh-ROKE) a style of 17th-century architecture.

bigamy (BIG-uh-me) having two wives or husbands at the same time.

commune (KOM-yewn) a community in which the land is owned by a group rather than by individuals.

dissent (diss-ENT) disagreement with established government ideas.

edifice (ED-i-fis) a large structure such as a building or organization.

element (EL-uh-ment) the simplest part into which something can be divided.

embankment (em-BANK-ment) raised earth built to confine a canal.

eulogize (YU-luh-jize) to praise someone.

exploit (eks-PLOYT) to demand unjust profit from another's work.

illiterate (il-LIT-er-it) unable to read or write.

inorganic (in-or-GAN-ik) concerned with substances that are not organic, such as minerals.

journalist (JUR-nul-ist) a writer who works for a newspaper or magazine.

molecule (MAH-leh-kewl) the smallest amount of a chemical compound that has all the characteristics of that compound.

neoclassical (nee-oh-KLASS-ih-kul) related to the revival of a classic style.

organic (or-GAN-ik) concerned with carbon compounds, including living things.

Glossary (cont'd)

oppression (oh-PRESH-un) unjust or cruel treatment.

patience (PAY-shuns) a game of solitaire in which cards are laid out in order.

pedagogical (ped-uh-GODJ-ih-kul) having to do with teaching.

periodicity (peer-ee-oh-DISS-i-tee) the characteristic of repeating at intervals.

progressive (pro-GRESS-iv) in favor of positive political changes.

prophet (PRAH-fit) someone who foretells the future.

quota (KWOH-tuh) a limit set on the number of persons permitted to do something.

serf (SURF) a laborer owned by an estate.

solitaire (SOL-i-tayr) any of several card games played by one person alone.

specific gravity (spuh-SIFF-ik GRAV-ih-tee) the ratio between the weight of a set amount of a substance and the same amount of water.

spectroscope (SPEK-truh-skope) an instrument that breaks light into a color spectrum.

spectrum (SPEK-trum) the band of colors resulting from light passing through a prism.

symmetrical (sim-MET-ri-kul) having the quality of being well balanced.

tuberculosis (tuh-bur-kew-LOW-sis) an infectious disease that formerly was nearly always fatal but can now be controlled by inoculations.

valence (VAY-lents) the ability of an atom to combine with other atoms to form compounds.

For Further Reading

For Young Adults:

Evernden, Margery. "Dmitri Mendeleyev, Creator of the Periodic Table," *The Experimenters: Twelve Great Chemists.* Greensboro, North Carolina: Avisson Press Inc., 2001.

McGowan, Tom. *Chemistry: The Birth of a Science.* New York: Franklin Watts, 1989.

Works Consulted:

Brock, William H. *The Chemical Tree: A History of Chemistry.* New York: W.W. Norton & Company, 1992.

Horvitz, Leslie Alan. *Eureka! Scientific Breakthroughs that Changed the World.* New York: John Wiley & Sons, Inc., 2002.

Levere, Trevor H. *Transforming Matter: A History of Chemistry from Alchemy to the Buckyball.* Baltimore: The Johns Hopkins University Press, 2001.

Strathern, Paul. *Mendeleyev's Dream: The Quest for the Elements.* New York: St. Martin's Press, 2000.

Leicester H.M. , *The Historical Background of Chemistry,* Dover, New York, 1956, pp. 192-198.

Mazurs E.G., *Graphic Representations ofthe Periodic System During One Hundred Years,* Univ. Alabama Press, University, Alabama, 1975.

Mendeleyev Dmitri, *The Principles of Chemistry,* 3rd English Ed., Longmans, Green, and Co., London, 1905.

On the Internet:

Mendeleyev University of Chemical Technology: Dmitry Ivanovich Mendeleyev
http://www.bgsu.edu/departments/chem/MUCT/Mendeleyev.html

Woodrow Wilson Leadership Program in Chemistry: Dmitri Ivanovich Mendeleev
http://www.woodrow.org/teachers/ci/1992/Mendeleev.html

Index